BURNTWATER

poems by

Chee Brossy

Finishing Line Press
Georgetown, Kentucky

BURNTWATER

Copyright © 2021 by Chee Brossy
ISBN 978-1-64662-417-1 First Edition
All rights reserved under International and Pan-American Copyright Conventions. No part of this book may be reproduced in any manner whatsoever without written permission from the publisher, except in the case of brief quotations embodied in critical articles and reviews.

ACKNOWLEDGMENTS

I thank the editors of the following publications in which some of these poems have appeared, sometimes in earlier forms and under different titles:

The Denver Quarterly, American Indian Culture and Research Journal, Sentence Magazine, and *The Taos Journal of International Poetry and Art.*

Publisher: Leah Huete de Maines
Editor: Christen Kincaid
Cover Art and Design: Stacy Brossy
Author Photo: Renae Lee

Order online: www.finishinglinepress.com
also available on amazon.com

Author inquiries and mail orders:
Finishing Line Press
PO Box 1626
Georgetown, Kentucky 40324
USA

Table of Contents

Burntwater 1

Do We Still Pollen Young Pines 5

Heiau 7

Quilting 8

Coral 9

Carson City, 1957 10

Four Dogs 11

The House at Long Cornfield 12

Owl and the Sabre 14

Backbone 15

Homemade Ice Cream 16

And the Butterflies 18

Coronation 19

Atop Tó Adin Mesa 21

For my family

BURNTWATER

T'ááłá'í

The Hopis rode through here built a fire from the oak and scrub cedar by the water the stream or pool now they call it Burntwater old women cooking around a fire. My great grandmother cooked in the summer sitting her knees on the ground skirt spreading out steel grill laid over an open fire in shade house bits of dough crusting her fingers. Now a young woman cooks potatoes over a blue flame on a stove in her city apartment. Dohí dohí before you light the acetylene torch to imagine fire shot from the sky my grandfather says before soldering bezel to silver bracelet loved one then sealing copper tubing with the same torch where the water's leak busted frozen last night. I say I don't know how to light a fire. Tightly wound nylon holds the gas when I work it now over a large piece but the solder doesn't flow metal blackens the thatched roof has caught spark my love. When I call my grandfather Shicheii he answers hello Shicheii we share the name. Blackest metal driest winter swing the sun low behind glass windows bottle green sculptures. I taped him set the tape recorder between us on the table loved one do you understand the red light to catch every inflection throat clearing gravel.

Naaki

He said   My uncle killed a man by the train tracks in winter another tribe or white man brought his pistol. Trains stopped for the night he had to pay or he had to run I don't know how he came to the ceremonies after that. From the police or from the killing. I'd see his face in the spring firelight as pairs of men and women danced a slow step around the fire wrapped in blankets the men wearing cowboy hats tilted up off their right ear so they could lean their heads close to the women. My uncle watched without watching sang without singing.

He said She jumped off the cliff ran and jumped off the cliff. One soldier leapt from his horse to stop her my great grandmother said (we called her nihimá mother) to round us up set fire to our squash and melon fields smoke and ash like a summer fire but bitter in your heart. They found us campfire morning eating in the low piñons surrounded on horseback blue coats and brass buttons. Father shot first a snap in his neck bullet through forehead (she points) then fleeing rifle fire everyone dead and crying. Only my little mother and I brisk spring morning air cold in my throat cold and alive. We had almost made it to the canyon and shelter pine sap sticks to your teeth you taste its mint in every meal so they are the same food corn meal prairie dog yellow gourd use a strand of hair to pull pieces from crevices in your molars. Birds sing flit from tree to tree ahead of you as though it were any day. Come to the canyon's edge with the soldiers dragging us tied with rope. She breaks free. Where is the order of the sun indifferent meaning beats down on us she is fluid in these last steps the trees melting into rock at the edge and leaps. The sun is too bright everything flat and hard but she floats out. I miss her already. My little mother had stopped crying hours before she ran. I only heard my own tears. Now down. The sun's cords touching the rock at the edge meant she was gone.

He said   We met at the Indian school. A dry Nevada with dry mountains where I make jewelry and signs high up on scaffolding red paint on the window pane shirt sleeves ripped off for dexterity yellow billboards on route sixty-six. The road goes on forever just like you said but Nevada

I can't see anymore like my eye has cracked Nevada has fallen through every way I look. Six children so they could play with each other girls and one boy. In Flagstaff I see racism course through the coffee shops and schools. My brother opened a jewelry supply downtown. A prayer mountain on the north side Dookʼoʼoslííd we call it. They made their own games drew them on cardboard I said I'd paint them. The winters would have our truck spinning. I do not know what to say to my children. The road is hungry no matter how many signs you paint or politicians you work for their visions shouted in fists broken on mobs of our own people. Marriage is hard but that doesn't matter. Back to Gallup always inching closer to home but never reaching it we did it for you is what I say. Place with the big stone chimney they call Gamerco so many places we lived but always you children played where did you play? Where did you play? Turn off the tape turn off the tape turn off.

Táá'

To play in the mist this is the most important thing. The house we sit in is a hogan attached to a four-walled home old magazines from the 80s and 90s on the bottom shelves. Old western movie video tapes under the TV in faded sleeves. If you drive north of the house on the dirt road over the rolling hills of piñon trees sagebrush and tea get down from your truck and walk west over low cacti the earth is sandy almost like the ocean's edge and water used to cover us you can still find white shells. You will find Burntwater grove of trees and cedars yellow sandstone emerging from the loose earth in places where the Hopis camped and let their horses drink. But in the house in the hogan where the skylight soft sun midmorning my grandfather cries and wipes tears from his face. His fingers look strange old and out of place against the face he rubs every morning to clear his eyes. I click the machine between us on the table slow but the echo of a gunshot and wait. We'll stop here today. To the south the freeway rumbles trucks haul refrigerators and pipes. On the windowsill the metal stamps and thin brushes sprout from rusted cans. It's cold. Even with the sun shining through the skylight I'll have to build a fire.

DO WE STILL POLLEN YOUNG PINES

Do weeds still choke the stream at Black Rock Spring
Is the water still cold
Is the dog unfed tied to a tree
Is it still muddy
Have grasshoppers eaten the field or deer

Do chainsaws still roar
Does the chain still bite
Does Alice shake her can of rocks
Does the old home still stand
Has the mud been blown away
        between the logs to leave it skeleton

Are the cows gone from the stock trailer
        their shit still caked
Does she visit every summer
        our new home with old logs
Does the hummingbird ever get out
Is horny toad still spiked
        in our hands, our throats

Do we threaten *They come at night*
        and take your hair
Is the house still half-built
Do we still pollen young pines
        praying for height
Do bottles glint with sun
Does mountain lion walk above us

Does the truck still kick up
        a fine silt when we come through with a shovel
Does bread still curl on the grill
Are we still burning our children in the den
Are we still searching for the Twins
Has Reyonda come home or Daryl

Does water still gush from the spring's pipe
Do we still fistfight for water
Does the circle of juniper branches stand from last year
Do we still see her bumping through the woods
Does wind still sound
thick and roaring through those trees?

HEIAU

I have never smelled the rank fur musty smell of bear. Only once in my life have I ridden a horse—in Hawaii on the north shore where a small sunburnt lady settled her four-horse corral. If Eddie stops to eat on the trail she hollered it's because he's forgotten you're on his back—in all that leafy greenness thick coily roots and reedy trunks turning sharp ridges velvet the smells rich with old earth overripe like the mangoes that fell in our driveway in August oozing into dark red soil and the world of ants. What a horse I whisper *shilíí'* I'm still here and he never steps off the trail. *Shilíí' hazlíí'*—my horse has appeared, has come into being. We saunter clopping to where a hill of lava rocks rises jagged with air holes air of people we will never know a silence inside silence the sea horizon blue. In their Honolulu apartments the whitewash gone yellow and outside on balconies their yellowing surfboards rusted bicycles their cars crackling in the sun and I think of my own car fading in my desert the paint flecking away until it is a skeleton whispering for another ride.

Deer this morning beside the road big ears skinny head bent low to the shoots of green sprung up around what once was Red Lake now a green and yellow field of weeds the deer calling plunge your heads into the willows choking the stream. *Bįįh* means deer but what did it mean before the Apaches split from us to live in teepees and sing water drum songs, dance arm in arm. Still we talk in our language because we know they'll understand. The old Hawaiians carried all those rocks *Heiau* and watched them for movement remembering their own journey across the ocean. A woman gets up to sing in the thick morning air full of flower horse sweet rot and far away coming high on the wind the salty smell of ocean opening over the rocks the trade winds. Time to push boat into bay into surf beyond whitecaps flaring the horizon ripples and far away visible just below the clouds the ghost of an island.

QUILTING

Four children play WWE in a patch of dirt they've outlined and softened with a spade. But hardness remains and the oldest girl cries when slammed to earth by her little sister.

The fort grows hot this summer, cookie pans warming. Thanksgiving and we miss even the troublemakers, the mean aunties, but most guiltily those who are gone, who, alive, we bore as burdens.

Together we ready our garden, cutting and opening fences, then wait for our uncle with the tractor.

A bomber flies low over the school and everyone—students and teachers and lunch ladies—stops to look up.

A woman weaves and stitches, breaks, picks it up again. For months, crying sometimes. She wipes her face when she comes to the scene of soldiers roping children together by their necks,

shooting mothers when they try to stop them—some lie bloodied on the ground—the barracks nearby full of chained, raging fathers. They have no faces, but the mothers reach, always reaching, all we can see of fathers are their arms, their hands.

Why remember? *Best to forget*, they said. But as there are welders and teachers, singers and scientists, so rememberers, too.

Gorman Hall, site of the Navajo Fair Art Show: across from the quilt, a young man sells his comic books. Leaning in when asked about his robots, his superheroes. Why do they look white? *I know*, he says. *I'm trying to change that.*

On a cloudy winter day, a father chops wood. The thud reaches us late, long after the blow, bouncing first off the clouds.

CORAL

Woman's choice, this dance. Afterwards, he took his pocketknife and cut from around his neck a string of coral beads. For you, he said, thank you.

The next night he came again; she could tell he was looking for her and couldn't hide his smile when she asked again.

In the end she had enough for a necklace. But he went off with Manycattle to fight them and she never heard from him again.

Strangers warned them. They'd come riding through the mountain constantly looking back, stopping just long enough to say, They're after us, we've been all the way from Ch'ooshgaii already.

There were only two horses. They decided that her sister and her niece would take them and she would go on foot. Before they left, hurried, the few sheep running circles in the corral, she gave the manystrand necklace to her niece-daughter. Keep this with the Tó'aheedlíiniis, she said—not saying *if I don't come back*—and put it over her daughter's head and hugged her.

They went eventually to the canyons and never saw their sister, their little mother again.

They heard she was captured and imprisoned in the Crying Plain, but they couldn't find her and never knew where she died.

Then my mother gave it to me. Before any others she sought me out. I was between husbands, and she said, I have something for you, it is a responsibility and maybe it will settle you down.

And now I give it to you, niece-daughter, because you show some quality of that woman, making your own decisions, standing up to your uncles. Look how it shines, polished by wear, the color pale, nearly orange. Breathe it, that no one will say it doesn't belong to you.

CARSON CITY, 1957

Pale yellow walls trellis around the sink mirror she eases the door closed slumps to the tiled floor. Breathe breathe breathe the children out playing and yelling. Crying pricked by the tacks holding carpet to kitchen floor her shoulder against the door. The asphalt cicada din presses around her mountains bursting highway heaving up neighbors waving in the sun smiles chiseled into their faces eyebrows sewn on with a broken machine. Their clothes flowered socks blue topstitching on a man's trousers but she can't see their heads for the glare. She blinks and the sun jumps overhead here where mountains descend and cacti burst from the cracked ground. Water water water. The cars snake tracks in the dirt the vinyl interior inflates pressing into her face. The felt tacking on the roof sags and wraps around her tongue. Who will save her at the house? The man at work going deaf in a blue hole jackhammering a new bank casino warehouse. Carries the machine wail home in his mouth. No. The children cry heaving sobs and her face crumbles. Catches it in the trellis mirror the lines around her mouth and red brick. She was a majorette. The wall lists to the right lists until the ceiling flips. Say it. The walls swallow. Say it. Citrus smell of shiver and sweat. *She came over the mountain singing sing sing* she wraps her arms around herself tucks her dress under. *She looked out over the prairie dogs the crying prairie dogs the wind bending the yucca fruit low.*

FOUR DOGS

You wake to the plain cut by early stars. First you must remove the dogs, four of them skittering around the shed and juniper trees. Call them, hold your hand out and pick them up under their muscular bellies, hoist each into the pickup bed where their claws clack, until they stand looking at you warily, ears up, dipping their shoulders. Collarless, fit from running, hunting, following horses, trained to be called to a stop when they see sheep. Though he omits the possessive, they are the boy's dogs.

The boy who'd been riding that day with his cousin the young bullrider with the quick smile and stutter. They had been roping and riding the neighbor's cows. Their boots caked with drying mud. The dogs will stay while you enter the hogan for the final sing, last one before sunrise, before gray and then blue-lighted stars. Your in-laws told you, The dogs are running around, and you understood why it was important you do this small duty amid an intricate ceremony. Water, charcoal, ash. If you can find young bullriders who still help.

Night: first, stars prick the curtain, then swimming dark and dogs go quiet—who can recall them from deep night? Finally last quiet, last silence before birds return from the north. The singing picks up even as you tire, grey morning rolling through the doorway, where the blankets have been pulled back, the dogs beside the truck now, waiting. We walk without jackets to the plowed ground, there to dump the water.

THE HOUSE AT LONG CORNFIELD

We skirt mesas in Hopi land, view sandy plains, blue valleys and distant San Francisco Peaks, short houses hanging off cliff's edge—Shungopavi, Oraibi, then down into fields, Moenkopi. Minds in the mood for travel, returning to red, to blue trees cottoning. A white dog sits on the shoulder, head laid on paws until we pass, traffic on a Saturday.

I believe they helped us plant corn. And, neighboring, we visited their medicine men, their language like water running down sandstone. Route 66, Interstate 40, were dirt roads winding up the mesa. Even the trails to Fort Sumner that became billboards flaking in fifty years of sun.

We race with them first as children, now as men and women up mesas, down arroyos, kicking rocks, leaping cacti. After this summer's race in honor of Tewanima, Hopi Olympian, I hunched over, hands on my knees. The stone steps we'd climbed in the last mile took everything, the people hanging over the edge shouting in water language. I gulped mouthfuls from a plastic bottle then splashed the rest on my face until water ran into the dirt, where it pooled before sinking. A boy with a braid let go of his father's hand, ran up and kicked dirt on my feet, then glared at me. In front, his hair was cut into fringe. As the announcer called the winners, I realized he'd covered the water. His dad, with the same hairstyle, laughed at us both.

This was before we drove back through Chilchinbeto, changed, before we stopped in Kayenta and you talked with a grandmother who spoke only Navajo, who scolded us for joining too soon after the ceremony—we couldn't sit on the same bed in her house. Still, she called me Son when we said goodbye. This was before we got stuck in Many Farms' purple clay, before we sat in an old hogan between Black Mesa and Navajo Mountain where people used to camp among junipers and orange sand on their way to Kayenta or *Tónaneesdizí* or a nine-night sing. A place called *Dá'ák'eh Haneezí*—Long Cornfield. That field is gone now, but some people still name it, touching the age-old, the time-worn.

There was another dog beside the road in Hopi, bent at its work, clamping and pulling. It looked up as we drove by, then turned back to what lay there—carcass of another dog. We passed into their land of flat-roofed houses, netless basketball hoops, and there, standing alone, were four poles, wire fencing falling away—the remains of a backstop. And though it was empty then, they must still play, tossing the ball, runners on base, crack of a bat, fans honking their horns flashing their lights—but for us it was empty and January then, the last snowfall not yet melted when we drove through on our way, though we didn't know it yet, to the house at Long Cornfield.

OWL AND THE SABRE

Bíhoosh'aah: learning, to learn, I am learning something, (**ł'aah*): to push a solid, round object (SrO), and thereby make space within yourself for a language, system, skill.

In Mexico, husband and wife are "love" around a dinner table. Pass the soup of shrimp, my love, administer mango yogurt, my love, plait my hair, *mi amor*, give me your scalp-scent, for tonight I desire to walk the festival's streets, to roam the *Zócalo*, to traffic, my hands full when a salesman strums his classical guitar *Handmade* he will say *just for you*.

They tell me *Indians will be out tonight*. I will have their corn stew with chile and lime. Let's forget others we have called *Love* forget we ever knew them, *conocer*: to know, to have known, to be saturated with.

In the Fearing Time, south of Socorro, a woman escaped her Spanish-Mexican enslavers—*tú la conoces*. Travelling only at night, she encountered wolves and fought them with a cavalry sabre. *Se escapó*. On the third night of running, of praying—*sodilzin*—an owl hoots and she stops. Her next step would be into the precipice. Who knows how far she would fall, how deep the canyon goes, if into trees, rocks, or water? She can feel gravity looming. But for the owl and sabre she would have fallen into wolves that night, to know, to have known, to be familiar with.

BACKBONE

The stream turns brown and birds go quiet, then, as irrigation into
    a field, the river turns, a yellow blanket thrown across from
    bank to bank. The Chairman holds the murky water in a clear
    mug, examines it in sunlight, then kneels and dips again, as
    though trying to catch something.

A stinkbug crosses the road, the sun shining purply off its back, and
    flips when a car whooshes over it.

The wild turkeys of autumn flap their way into a Ponderosa, shedding
    feathers, but without calling. A bobcat runs at the edge of
    headlights along the gravel road, then veers and leaps onto a
    cottonwood stump and watches the truck rumble by.

The line at a food stand backs up and up, disrupting oncoming traffic
    at the flea market, and people get angry. *What's the holdup?*
    Someone says. *They ran out of sheep intestine, so they sent
    somebody to the store.*

The tribal college president walks through the cubicles, sees a woman
    whispering to her friend and thinks everyone is out to get her,
    all these small, rude people, gunning, shooting her down.

*They were grooming me to be a leader, he tells his son, and I disappointed
    all of them. But hey, I still rodeo.*

A truck whistles weightless over the washboards, rain ignites the
    sagebrush field, the watermelon huge in the yard, on their way
    to have a say on the fences.

A backbone, my backbone, the ripple in sandstone.

HOMEMADE ICE CREAM

What I didn't say:
The escaping woman was pregnant.

Sitting on a bench at the Railyard,
my expectant friend listens to live music.
Someone sells homemade ice cream
out of a deep, frosty bin.
Look at it move, she says.
When the music gets too loud it moves.
She leans back so sun shines
on her rounded T-shirt.
But I'm too scared to touch it.
It's crazy, she says. *Did you see?*
I don't know what I saw.

If we sacrifice our children
for the good of the People what then?
Are we selfish or caring?

Because the woman with the sabre
had no milk, she couldn't care for her baby.
No milk, no food to make it.
If they don't live to smile
with unrepeatable joy, at mother
behind the camera, sitting
on auntie and uncle's lap.
It's easy to be afraid.

When are the dances?
Already! she says. *Where were you?*
I'd like some ice cream, but it will take
too long. Already we shout
over the screaming electric guitar.
I've got to go, I say, even though I don't.
She looks disappointed, *Already?*
Waiting through this act for the next.

We wrap our children in our arms,
squeeze them as they squirm from us,
dress them in winter coats,
button their little Hawaiian shirts.
They jump into pools awaiting our catch,
smiling big until the splash makes them
blink because they had our milk.

Looking back, I see my friend has turned
to her sister, arranging who will wait
for homemade ice cream.

AND THE BUTTERFLIES

She will come back in other ways, they said. You won't know at first, looking out at the sunrise, sunset, mountains in winter, a bird winging its way from the woodpile.

I want to say, Please come back, Mother. But I can't, I don't. It will take a long time. Everything will remind you: your car won't start, huffing like her old truck. Running the trail after work, you'll see a butterfly and know. Crying right there in the middle, tears dripping into dirt.

Everyone came for advice: sisters, brothers, even if they'd been fighting, broken when a husband left, when dreams wouldn't allow sleep, when they feared lightning. She had many friends, from her young days, to her political days, to her prayer woman days—they called on her. Strangers drove to her house for help, hearing of this woman.

She visited Bolivia with her son to teach textiles. Around a coca leaf fire, dressed in woven hats and bright serapes, their medicine men whispered, *We saw you come in, like a wave crashing. For a moment we were afraid.* But she hadn't come to hurt them. Her own prayers joined theirs.

And I was envious of them all. These people taking her time, taking what she gave them. But I am your daughter, your first-born, your Warrior girl, and I miss you. *Be patient,* she says, *you always hurry.* Now all I have are sunrises, sunsets, wind through juniper, butterflies. And they were right.

CORONATION

Smell horses between us. Bring the fair
dust in your hair, the taste of machined curleyfries.

Atop the Ferris wheel rocking *Do not rock the seat.*
See all the rides: a child's overturned box of toys.

To the south, rodeo lights, the grounds dusting up—
unbroken, roped horses fresh from the mustang roundup

in the wild horse race. The time the neighborhood strays
got together and killed the tame ones,

pouring yard to yard, weaving through shrubbery
and chain link fencing.

After the horse race, coronation.
Holding hands, stealing through a dust storm, through the powwow
    stands.

Mica streaks chalky on sandstone, on sidewalk.
Every person's pain is their own, like measuring a handful of flour.

In spring 1990, we can't park under the shade trees
because of all the broken glass. Inside a truck's metal tank,

footsteps chase you, clanging off the walls.
In the evening, at dinner, you were asked: Frybread or tortilla?

Just before night falls, the carnival lights come on,
The Zipper clangs and shakes, pealing with screams.

At the rodeo grounds the queen gives her acceptance speech
in Navajo. Was that a story about her grandparents? Her dog?

How he howled and howled when they left him.
After the coronation, the Apaches will go out,

marching from the bull gate, led by
their crowned dancers, then women dancers in calico

then lead singer with drum, his backup singers.
And finally you will step down the stands

onto uneven, plowed rodeo ground,
link arms with the arcs of people, and join them.

ATOP TÓ ÁDIN MESA

In fly swarms of mosquitos,
foreign wasps, cooped origami cranes
flap their heavy, oiled wings,
a press of maladies: first wind, then malaria,

then all the accusations of thievery
in border town department stores, all the fights
at stoplights, the deaths by exposure.
Still, there are protectors in the pollen:

blue, red, and green, nights when snowstorm
rages dark as the ocean deeps and hide twangs
inside a cabin, long-stick music, a gloved dance.
In the wood, a grandfather and granddaughter

are confronted by a bear. It rears snorting, roaring.
Wherefore the man speaks to it, firmly, clearly,
in Navajo: which camp they're going to and why.
Because you must have faith, you must announce your designs.

The snowstorm knocks at the door.
The bear walks away.
We climb stringed light, through corpuscular caves,
broken thoughts and fissured boulders, three sentences

gone wild, winter taking too long to arrive.
Atop *Tó Ádin* mesa we run,
feet slapping the washboards, breathing fine silt
and girlfriend thoughts, dimpled smiles behind our eyelids,

Three Flowers Brilliantine trickling down our scalps,
and we wish to smell their hands,
the sweat between their breasts.
Listen to their crescendoing laughter.

The Tribal Peacemaker has come, hands clasped
behind her back, thoughts hidden behind whirlwinds
while the boy drinks bleach, while the ankle swells
and purples and our brothers run on without us.

We've been auditioning for a play—
with wigs, with artificial limbs and smiles,
painted-on wrinkles, an eye patch, an imaginary cane.
To those of us who've always shaved our heads I say

Wait, when the man lays out his starched clothes,
wait. Because there is only one size,
and it's too big. There is only one drab color
and it is oppressive.

The Peacemaker watches, still, she listens.
Shaped from mud. For some, the clay
has become brittle. For others it's fired
and tempered with mica—their hearts burn

long and slow, people we warm ourselves to.
Others are still wet, an examining thumbprint
at their lips. Others are sealed with a shiny resin,
a shield, and very few find their way inside.

These are golds, these are emeralds,
this is coral inlaid into the body,
into eyes, eardrums, and whorls.
Stacks of books, infant footprints, wood carvings,

busted bicycles, worn out friends, wool blankets,
pictures hidden inside. Leaves have begun to fall,
but it's still warm, so is it memory?
The transformation: green, yellow-green,

gold, amber, rust; you remember
the annual sorrow. It is good to be sorrowful,
to hear hushed leaves settling, the tick
of stems breaking, wind gusting its percussion.

Chee Brossy was born in Chinle, Arizona, and grew up in Red Mesa, Arizona. He is Diné, originally from Lukachukai and Wheatfields, Arizona. He attended Dartmouth College where he studied English and Native American Studies. His poetry has appeared in *Denver Quarterly, Sentence Magazine, Red Ink Magazine* and elsewhere. Stories from his collection *Goat's Milk* have been published in *Kenyon Review Online* and *PRISM International*. His first full-length collection *The Strings Are Lightning And Hold You In* is forthcoming from Tupelo Press in 2022. He has worked as a reporter, basketball coach, English literature instructor, and archivist. He lives in New Mexico.

www.ingramcontent.com/pod-product-compliance
Lightning Source LLC
LaVergne TN
LVHW041521070426
835507LV00012B/1737